For you and me, too!

ANIMAL-KIND

Pablo Salvaje

Prestel
Munich • London • New York

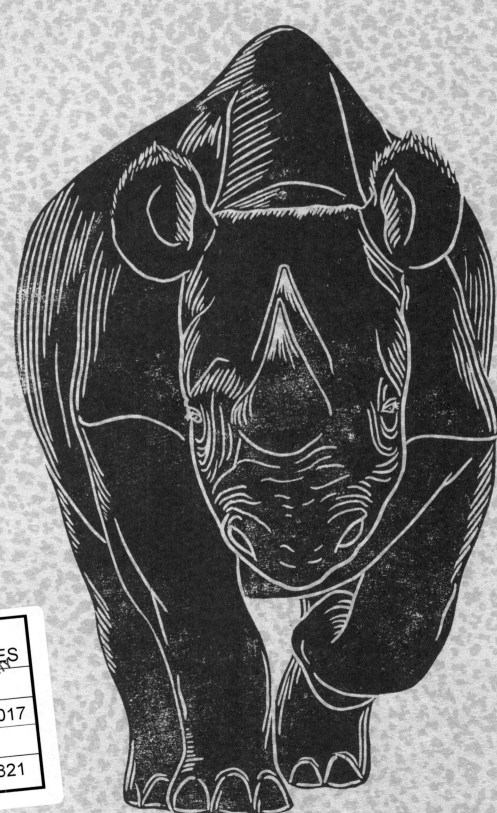

FOREWORD

People and animals live all around planet Earth. We share our world
with millions of creatures, each one more fascinating than the other.
Every living being is made up of atoms and molecules. Together, all of us
make up a framework of life that is in harmony with its environment.
We all live and breathe on the same globe. The behaviour of every single
being should be respected.

Mother Nature has equipped each life with a soul. Our soul makes us
unique. It is there to help us come to terms with ourselves and our
relationship to other species. Those who examine their soul will be filled
with understanding, compassion and respect. They will recognize that
every living creature is different from ourselves and therefore deserves
to be protected and nurtured.

Your soul is the secret that unites all species. It is the mainstay of a life
whose many, many layers are yet to be uncovered. In this book, we'll
discover, with each and every image, the souls of Others. We'll do this
by taking a close look at the way other creatures feel and the amazing
things they are able to do. Then, we will come to understand that we
are all part of a greater whole.

While you are reading these pages, dozens of cranes will set off on
their travels, leaving the cold snow and migrating to less frosty regions.
Countless schools of whales will communicate with one another through
song, which is something they have perfected over centuries of evolution.
Thousands of penguins will begin to mate and inhabit whole islands
with love. Millions of creatures will move forward with their lives.
They are all following a strong instinct, which enables them with hearts
pounding to perform unbelievable feats on a daily basis. This is the way
life has been throughout centuries of time, and it's the way nature has
always meant it to be.

The soul has led us to create the book you now have in your hands. Let's
dive in together and explore the world of nature. Let's learn about the
mannerisms, quirks, history and truths of the animal soul that is in each
and every one of us.

LOVE

Love is a word that means so much. We use it in countless ways to show how we feel about each and every thing. Life is all about love: sensing it and showing it.

Love is free. It reveals itself in a variety of ways when animals interact with one another, regardless of whether there are only two of them or a family of twenty. Love is not just a strong feeling or a simple passionate moment.

Love is what motivates us in life. It is a universal energy that moves us to do everything and beyond. It is a bond uniting us, and it's reason enough for us to move mountains and cross rivers just to find the ideal partner and the right moment to reproduce. Love moves us to find food for our young so that they can become big and strong and go their own way. Notice how penguin parents love and care for their young, even in the coldest parts of the planet. Love fills the soul. It gives every living thing structure and shape. Without a soul we would not receive love, and without love we would not even be here today.

Giraffes, flamingos, sea unicorns, tortoises, rhinoceroses, you and me: every single one of us feels love. Depending on the type of animal, the sense of love can be brief, deep, life-long or as variable as the seasons. Yet it remains pure, true and free. All creatures prosper with love. Rowdy mating rites show off the beauty that each creature has by nature. The male peacock reveals its seductive feathers with the sole aim of reproducing – and thus remaining an important part of the universe of living organisms. Every mating strategy has the same goal: to ensure that the greatest number of offspring can live long enough to have offspring of their own. This means that love is not just an instinct, but something we cannot do without if we are to continue living and evolving on our planet.

RHYTHMS

The earth we walk on is in constant motion, with a rhythm as regular as the beat of your heart. It is a living organism, functioning like a clock, with an internal tick-tock-tick-tock that keeps us connected and invites us to dance. Every animal is guided by its very own rhythm, which is as familiar and true as the return of springtime. Some animals are early risers: sloths and koalas wake up when the sun rises and enjoy every watchful movement in the greenery. Others revel in the night. The stars accompany the night owls and eagle owls during their silent nighttime excursions for food. Elephant herds use the twilights of both morning and evening to wander off along thousands of miles of elephant tracks toward faraway places, seeking out watering holes in the very hottest months. Each of these animals lives with different rhythms, yet all are in unison with one another.

SURVIVAL

Finding food is necessary for the survival of all animals. This continous struggle is sometimes won and sometimes lost. The art of survival requires lots of skill, whether on foot, flying or swimming. It also requires intelligence when camouflaging and a permanently sharp sixth sense when escaping from hunters. Predators have a lofty place in the food chain. But they are not always hunting other creatures. Crocodiles, for instance, can survive for up to a year without any food whatsoever. They are not just clever; they are patient, too. Survival takes more than being skillful at combat. Just look at the cooperation between the oxpecker bird and the buffalo. While the bird gets a meal of insects and ticks from the buffalo's back, the buffalo gets a thorough cleaning. This harmonious friendship helps both animals to survive and thrive.

In wilder regions of the Earth, such as the freezing-cold Arctic and Antarctic, the climate becomes another enemy to survival. Thick fur and a dense layer of fat save the polar bear. This is how it endures the icy temperatures and fits in with its surroundings – all with the goal of survival.

TRANS-FORMATION

At some point in its life, each creature experiences a temporary or permanent change that helps it to grow, protect itself from harm or regenerate. In short, it enables the animal to adapt to its environment. Transformation is the process by which this change comes about.

The transformation (or metamorphosis) experienced by a butterfly completely changes its body. After spending most of its life as a caterpillar in the foliage, it transforms into a winged beauty in the sky.

When exposed to predators, good camouflage can be the best defense. 'Stay motionless and become one with your surroundings' is the policy of the chameleon. This reptile also uses its talent for changing 'clothes' in order to express its feelings. By altering the color of its body, a chameleon can communicate with others – and even express whether it is happy or sad.

Animals can also transform by shedding their skin while growing or renewing parts of their bodies. Many reptiles, such as snakes, lose their skin several times throughout their lives when it becomes too small for them. Even though they neither lose their color nor their pattern, snakes must change their skin in order to rid themselves of the old and start anew.

Nature shows us that today we are neither what we were yesterday nor what we are going to be tomorrow. The strength to hold on to what is needed and to retain our identity is the wonderful magic of transformation.

HABITAT

Ancient, durable, stately and wise: trees stretch out to the skies like mighty, breathing skyscrapers. They provide a home for thousands upon thousands of other species. A whole host of animals can live in one single tree.

Just as nature determined it, forests extend across our whole planet like an enormous architectural masterpiece. They are the lungs of the earth. All tree creatures live in them together: from a tiny spider in its delicate nest to families of primates in the canopy. And as these communities grow larger, relationships are made and the most different of animals become all the more dependent on one another. Within this harmonious social web, every creature knows its place.

One single tree can offer refuge for hundreds of animals, regardless of whether they have feathers, scales or fur. A woodpecker will build the ideal nest for its eggs in the trunk of a tree. Squirrels look for food between the branches and twigs. And families of little animals, such as moles, create vast tunnelled homes around the roots.

When you explore the woods near your home town, you can get a good sense of how all creatures live together in our communal world.

WATER

Water is the source of life, an essential part of our being. It covers most of our Earth, and any form it takes is teeming with creatures. Huge oceans, rippling rivers, peaceful lakes and roaring waterfalls are all a part of our planet's environment, its circle of life. The enormous seas are home to an endless number of animals. Wonderful jellyfish that swim against the current without even a skeleton are among the oldest ocean inhabitants. Their bodies contain up to 95% pure water. Other creatures that are still more remarkable also occupy these depths.

As with the land, we can find fantastic examples of development, co-existence and survival in water. We discover genuine living communities in paradises below the ocean surface. Coral reefs, for example, house all kinds of species: from the tiniest fish who constantly fight for their own space, right up to the majestic humpback whales who only visit the reef once a year to have their young. It is a puzzling world and we only know a small amount about it. Nature has created many species here that people have not even discovered. Life under the seas is a constant evolution, and it's part of a story that started being written millions of years ago …

TREASURES

We also live alongside little gems of extraordinary tenderness; true masterpieces of nature that could fit into anyone's jacket pocket. Insects, molluscs, lizards and other tiny creatures make the most out of their small size in order to adapt to a planet inhabited by what they regard as giants. Despite their minuteness, they do not go unnoticed. Animals with decorated armor, rigid conches and sturdy snail shells, all of which serve as travelling homes, are harmless, sensitive beings with souls. They are able to build, serve and love, yet they also need our recognition and respect in order to be preserved. These tiny treasures with big souls make up only a fraction of all the life that is living around us. They are part of an invisible net connecting us all — on a place we call *Earth*.

REMINDERS

The dodo was a bird that once lived on the island of Mauritius, which lies off the southeast coast of Africa. It became extinct after humans brought animals to the island that devoured its eggs. What's more, the large dodo had such little wings that it couldn't fly, and so heavy a beak that it couldn't walk around nimbly. Nature certainly did not make things easy for the dodo. These pages should remind us of the dodo and all the other animals that no longer exist. Such animals deserve to be remembered hundreds of years after their disappearance – because they remain part of our reality today.

Saber-toothed cats, cave bears and dodos are just a few of the many animals that have been wiped out. It is through the course of nature that animals become extinct. But humans are speeding up this natural process. The changes we've made to our environment have reduced the diversity of species that share planet Earth.

EPILOGUE

Let's explore the story of creation page by page, examining the incredible masterworks of nature and learning how they live. That way, we can touch and understand other species and see how they deserve our respect and admiration. Our bond with other living beings will make us conscious of the impression we leave on this little planet, which exists in the middle of an endless universe.

Every single life form is vital and has good reason to be here. We are all part of a cloak that wraps itself protectively around the same soul. It is the duty of all right-minded people to preserve everything that comes across their path; to protect the Earth, which has been loaned to us; and to love all the creatures with which humans share the Earth.

People defend what they love, and love requires knowledge. Listen to your heart and your five senses. We are all part of the story we are living in right now. And what's more, many blank pages remain to be filled in the history of creation. Your inner instinct will help you to listen to the animal soul within you and to protect the Earth for future generations.

This book is dedicated to all mother elephants
who are role models with their unswerving
courage …,

to all penguin fathers who return home after
every heavy storm to show us that we need
security to survive,

to all female wolves looking after their pack
and howling wildly at the moon, which
attracts us and draws us together,

to all gorillas who look after each other, love
one another and play happily in the deepest
jungle every single morning,

to all our descendants, because it's their
enthusiasm that has opened our eyes to believe
everything is possible,

and to all of those no longer with us and to
you, because you make my heart beat faster.

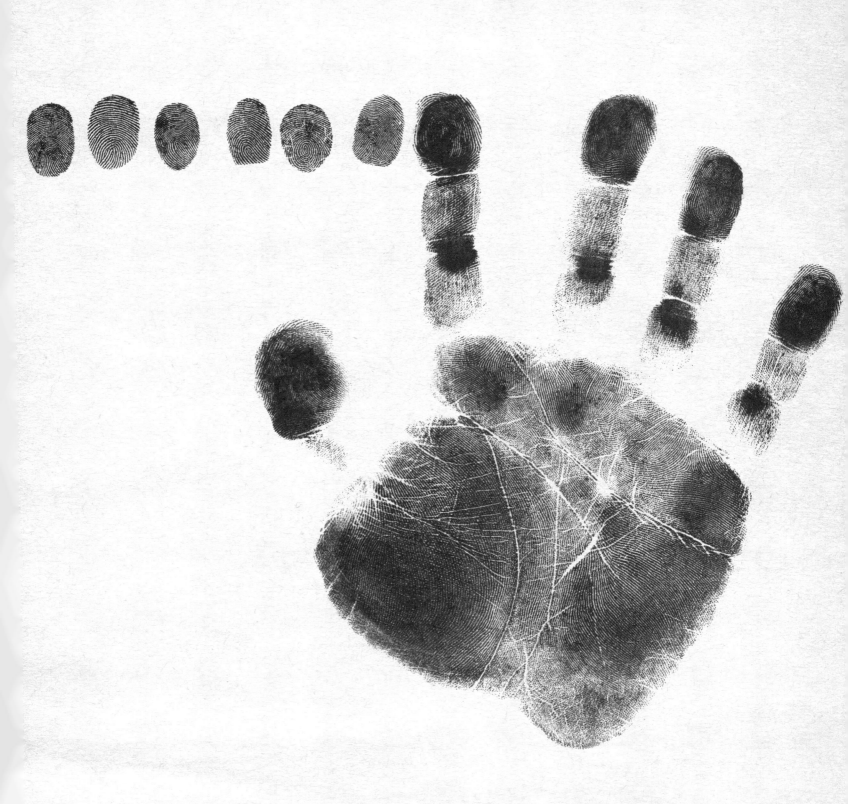

Pablo Salvaje does not work with his hands, but with his heart.

He was born in Seville, Spain and had constant access to the world of print from an early age. The noise from the huge machines in his parents' old print shop – and their breathtaking way of printing at high speed – aroused his passion for ink and paper.

As a journeyer and explorer, Pablo cites nature as his greatest source of inspiration. There is always a memory and a story to be uncovered in the logs, leaves and rocks he collects. His prints reveal their stories accordingly.

Mia Cassany, from the publisher Mosquito Books in Barcelona, discovered a hand-printed heart one day and was immediately inspired. Without hesitation, she met up with the artist Pablo Savaje, only to discover much more in his art than she had expected. Many soulful stories were concealed in his prints. Mia soon embarked on a book project that could best present Pablo's creations to others.

An adventure like this one required another artist to make a perfect team. The graphic skills and passion of **Anna Prats** provided color and form to the 300+ prints by Pablo on these pages. After a year of devoted work, the three of them were able to re-create nature's beauty with one clear aim: to help us better empathize with all the living things that share our planet.

ANIMALS IN THIS BOOK

Title page: Whale shark

Foreword: Black rhinoceros

Love: Flamingo
Family: Chinstrap penguins, Emperor penguins
Couple: Zebras
Courtship: Peacock

Rhythms: Red-crowned cranes
Silence: Sloths, Koalas
Night: Little owl, Eurasian eagle-owl, Barn owl, Great horned owl
Migration: African elephants, Barnacle geese

Survival: Common crane, Snake
Fighting: Crocodiles, Zebra, Giraffes, Oryx, Antelope
Symbiosis: African buffalo, Oxpeckers
Climate change: Polar bears

Transformation: Caterpillar, Cocoon, Butterflies
Metamorphosis: Frogs' eggs, Tadpoles, Frogs
Camouflage: Chameleons
Skinning: Snakes

Habitat: Spiders
Treetop: Spider monkeys
Tree trunk: Woodpecker, Tree squirrel, Bees
Roots: Ants, Fox, Meerkats, Raccoon, Jerboa, Badger, Pangolin, Hedgehogs, Nasua

Water: Octopus, Seahorse
Marine waters: Jellyfish
Coral reef: Spotfin lionfish, Clownfish, Moorish idol, Triggerfish, Emperor angelfish,
Pufferfish, Trumpetfish
Communication: Blue whale, Sperm whale, Humpback whales

Treasures: Anna's hummingbirds
Insects: Stag beetles, Dragonflies, Scarab beetles, Rosalia longicorns, Harlequin beetles,
Longhorn beetles
Protection: Indian star tortoise, Crab, Sea urchin, Common limpet, Scallop, Sea snails,
Snail, Green ormer, Nautilus, Common periwinkle, Mollusks, Mussels

Reminders: Dodo, Cave bear, Saber-toothed cat

© for the Spanish edition: 2017, Mosquito Books, Barcelona,
SL Ramón y Cajal 44 – 08012 Barcelona (Spain)
www.mosquitobooksbarcelona.com
Title of the original edition: Alma Animal

© for text and illustrations: 2017, Pablo Salvaje
Creative Director: Mia Cassany
Editorial Manager and Design: Ana Prats

© for the English edition: 2017,
Prestel Verlag, Munich · London · New York
A member of Verlagsgruppe Random House GmbH
Neumarkter Strasse 28 · 81673 Munich

Prestel Publishing Ltd.
14-17 Wells Street
London W1T 3PD

Prestel Publishing
900 Broadway, Suite 603
New York, NY 10003

Library of Congress Control Number: 2017938033
A CIP catalogue record for this book is available from the British Library.

Translation: Paul Kelly
Copyediting: Brad Finger
Production management: Corinna Pickart
Typesetting: textum GmbH
Paper: Golden Sun Woodfree

MIX
Paper from
responsible sources
FSC® C020056

Verlagsgruppe Random House FSC® N001967

Printed in China

ISBN 978-3-7913-7302-7

www.prestel.com